THE BLUFFER'S GUIDE TO BLUFFING

Mary Ellen Snodgrass
Peter Gammond

CENTENNIAL PRESS

The Bluffer's Motto

"Sincerity is everything.
If you can fake that, you've got it made."

George Burns

The Bluffer's Code

When tact and truth are not enough
The honest man must turn to bluff.

ISBN 0-8220-2200-1
U.S. edition © Copyright 1989 by Centennial Press
British edition © Copyright 1987 by The Bluffer's Guides

Printed in U.S.A.
All Rights Reserved

Centennial Press, Box 82087, Lincoln, Nebraska 68501
an imprint of Cliffs Notes, Inc.

INTRODUCTION

The **Bluffer's Guides** evolved in response to public demand one Sunday afternoon at The Rusty Nail during the writers' strike and has now grown from the original notion of having 10 titles toward a vision of expanding the series to include books on more than 3,567 subjects. This would provide a volume on virtually everything that a bluffer might want to bluff in—from simple topics that any fool can fake, such as politics and modern art, to the more obscure and baffling fields of computers and feminism.

A perceptive critic (and, remind me, we owe that guy a drink) summed up the whole principle and philosophy of big-time bluffery in one succinct statement:

> The Bluffer's Guides are literary proof that a little learning is a marvelous thing, and since that is all most of us are ever going to have anyway, we might as well get to know how to spread it thinly but effectively, like the last smidgen of peanut butter on the heel of the loaf.

The publisher, editors, writers, artists, maintenance crew, warehouse employees, and assorted hangers-on at Bluffer's Guides Central, together with printers, typesetters, and their factotums (or is it more correctly *factota*, after the Latin neuter nominative plural?) unanimously reject any reponsiblity for the recommendations within these volumes. Only the authors deserve blame, which doesn't seem fair, since they get so little out of it. But where is there fairness in this world these days, particularly to authors? Besides, authors thrive on abuse.

The staff expresses its thanks to the purchaser of these guides, but denies all damage to prestige and/or loss of respect in the community resulting from their purchase and use.

WARNING: The contents of this guide are dangerous and could cause permanent brain warpage. It should be read with tongue firmly in cheek. Note: While in this pose, do not engage teeth.

DEFINITION OF BLUFFING

bluff, *v.* 1674 (of unknown origin. Probably derived from an Algonquin term meaning "take cash, not beads.") Related to *bluff, adj.* (*i.e.* big, surly, blustering, fako) and evolving into its more familiar verb form meaning "to hoodwink by assuming a bold, fictitious façade."

1. *trans.* To trick or con. 2. In the game of *poker, q. v.* To induce an opponent to bet heavily to the point of giving up a perfectly bettable hand. 3. *intrans.* To attempt the act described in 2. Hence, **bluffer**, *n.*
(taken, with acknowledgment, from
The Shorter Oxford Dictionary)

bluff, *n.* A deliberate ruse, scam, or attempt to confuse an opponent.

bluffer, *n. ca.* 1650, a hostler or innkeeper. (Probably dial.) A deceiver who relies upon appearances. *cf.* References to national political conventions, televangelism, and circus acts.

bluffing, *n.* The feigning of a show of force where no real force exists; a phrase taken from the game of poker.
(from *Dictionary of Cardplayer's Slang*, 1989 edition)

The common poker usage expresses the intent of this series to a T. We prefer to avoid the terms "con" and "scam" in order to distinguish between the gentle art of bluffing and actual lying or cheating, which has never been our intent. Please note that a con artist is out for gain through deception; a bluffer merely wishes to keep the other fellow guessing.

The true aim of respectable bluffing is to hold your own on slippery ground, particularly when you are in the presence of a real authority, such as your boss, a blind date, or anyone who tries to make a fool out of you. The bluffer avoids being shown up or outwitted, especially by a pro. You can chalk up a win if you succeed in staring down your opponent or sidestepping a major disaster.

Scoring is part of the intrinsic joy of bluffing. Permit yourself a private snicker and one of the following awards:

- three points for besting experts, particularly if the competition is on their home turf—the nineteenth hole, a chamber music festival, or a chili cook-off.
- two points for a tie against an equal—a fellow bluffer who fails to convince and/or outbluff.
- one point if your opponent is clearly an idiot.

Note: Bluffers tend to score more ones than twos. Threes are extremely rare, probably because wise bluffers avoid placing themselves directly in harm's way.

In the current market, where bluffing is taken for granted, the simple bluff lacks pizzazz. For more oomph in your game, master the double-bluff and advance to the triple-bluff. The satisfactions far outweigh the dangers.

The **double** (or bi-bluff), a common practice; requires the bluffer to tell the truth as if it were a bluff.

The payoff: people think you're bluffing when you aren't.

The **triple** (or tri-bluff), a much more advanced technique; should only be attempted by masters of the first two levels, such as politicians, professional wrestlers, and aging sex goddesses. Here, the bluffer bluffs in the usual way so as to emulate the truth, but the truth itself is a bluff.

THE GENTLE ART
OF BLUFF

Why Bluffing Is Necessary

Our Plymouth Rock ancestors (*ca.* 1620) earned their neighbors' high regard if they

(1) knew a little bit about everything, from pushing plowshares to putting up chokecherry preserves;
(2) could fight Indians, either freestyle or from behind trees;
(3) figured out which tax collectors would accept a freshly plucked turkey in exchange for a paid-in-full receipt.

Times were less complicated for Captain John Smith and his gang. There hadn't been as much history as there has been since, and maps were still half empty. Nor had science really got going; nobody was expected to understand terminal displays, fax machines, or the time setting on a VCR. The arts in the Colonies were all pretty basic, ranging from sewing elaborate embroidery (no one ever surpassed Hester Prynne's *A*) to writing a multitude of doom-embellished sermons — masterpieces of sulfurous, equal-opportunity condemnation. A little learning was a dangerous thing.

The present-day American, by comparison, has so much to know that the chances of being more than

partially well-rounded (much less semi-circular) are slight. Even those who know everything there is to know about their chosen subjects (Norman Mailer on literature, Ronald Reagan on political ethics, Michael Jackson on nose jobs, Gloria Steinem on the E.R.A.) may be found sadly wanting in other departments.

At the same time, things are looking up for the ordinary person, whose means to self-improvement in any field of expertise is vastly more accessible than in Captain Smith's day. Ignorance is simply an admission of laziness. Successful conversationalists, especially those who read the Sunday supplement, like to appear *au courant* on most topics. They might not be genuinely interested in dialectical materialism, for example, or aerobics or missiles, but they might find themselves in a conversation on any of these subjects at a moment's notice. It's on these occasions that a careful manipulation of basic facts will help them bluff their way through any conversation with a reasonable degree of competency.

General Applications of Bluffing

Lest the average person get the wrong opinion, bluffery is more than the last resort of the ignoramus. The learned professor is no less in need of its face-saving effect than the sanitary engineer. Indeed, judicious bluffing is essential in covering gaps in what is supposed to be an infallible wealth of knowledge.

In **music**, for example, the general practitioner is constantly open to attack by the specialist — for example, the kind who knows all about the twelve-tone scale, the decline of rock since Lennon and Joplin, and developments in the Moog. The specialist, cashing in on a momentary advantage, will refuse to budge from an obvious area of expertise. Here the bluffer's knowledge of some diversionary facts (even fabricated data in desperate cases) will come in handy. The amateur must learn how to steer the conversation away from the specialist's home court and counterattack with any of the 3,566 subjects that the specialist knows little about.

Favorite subjects for bluffing used to be **politics, religion**, and **sex.** But these are not as popular as they once were. In fact, in some circles, such as Rotary clubs, cabinet meetings, the Vatican, and Little League, they are taboo. A recent survey reveals that the most talked-about subjects today, arranged in ascending order of importance, are money, teenagers, teachers' pay, money, foreign cars, waterbeds, cholesterol, Cancun, military preparedness, high-fiber diets, face-lifts, and money.

On occasion, bluffing can bail the bluffer out of a yawning black hole. For example, bluffing serves well

(1) as a means of self-defense at cocktail parties, in airport departure lounges, at class reunions, and during half-time;

(2) on used-car lots where glib salesmen quote superlatives from well-thumbed printed material;

(3) in certain professions, including law, real estate, police work, funeral directing, and insurance sales, where a degree of bluffing is essential to convince yourself and others that you know what you're talking about;

(4) in business (See Business);

(5) all the time. Bluffing isn't simply a game to be played at parties; it permeates your every waking moment.

How to Recognize a Bluffer

Certain physical idiosyncrasies differentiate bluffers from non-bluffers. The practiced or accomplished male bluffer may be recognized by the bland composure of his face and by the way he focuses on an invisible point in the middle of his challenger's forehead. The female of the species is deadlier in most ways and will often look an adversary straight in the eyes.

Professional bluffers (candidates for public office, strippers, or door-to-door vacuum cleaner sellers) use practical, perfected strategies for deception. They polish up every aspect of the art so that it's difficult to find chinks in their armor. When you face a state-of-the-art bluffer, you probably should, totally against your natural inclination, resort to the truth. On these occasions, it's best to keep a potent truth or two up your sleeve as a diversion, although you shouldn't overdo this ploy.

Casual or novice bluffers give themselves away by referring to small, inexpensive books in the palms of their hands. Don't let them see yours.

The Know-It-All and the Expert

If you're a regular bluffer, it's inevitable that you'll encounter a **know-it-all.** Here's someone that you'll have to treat with the utmost respect. To some degree, the know-it-all belongs under the genus *blufferus*, but with one clear distinction. Whereas true bluffers set out to *pretend* that they know what they're talking about, know-it-alls have a strong inner conviction that their opinions *are* the last word on any given subject. It's particularly difficult to deal with people when they actually *do* know what they're talking about. For your own protection, you should learn to detect right away that you're not simply dealing with a fellow bluffer with potentially superior skills.

The know-it-all leaves a trail as easy to follow as bread crumbs by

(1) talking to you as if you're a fool;
(2) exhibiting a limited sense of humor;
(3) supporting assertions with fact, a ploy that bluffers assiduously avoid;
(4) being on the other side of 50. After that milestone, as memory begins to fade, know-it-alls almost imperceptibly become bluffers. And generally very good ones.

Know-it-alls tend to thrive best in practical rather than artistic areas. They really shine at things like income tax (paying and evasion of), insurance, all aspects of business management, exotic cuisine, medical diagnoses, and travel – especially to places you never heard of.

What you must remember is that know-it-alls are *not* experts. They haven't indulged in anything as tedious as a lifetime study of any particular subject, but have simply accumulated masses of superficial knowledge from such sources as *Reader's Digest, Parade, National Geographic* specials, MacNeil-Lehrer, and *Consumer*

Reports. They come prepared with a ready answer, whatever the question. But they're easily trapped. Like most people, they worship as gospel almost anything in print or in the media. Because it comes from a remote source, they assume that it's carved on stone tablets. What they forget is that writers and programmers are themselves veteran bluffers.

Experts, on the other hand, are know-it-alls on only *one thing*. Their knowledge is therefore of greater magnitude and less open to question. You'll know an expert because he or she can tell you—indeed, will take special pains to inform you—that what *you* have read on their particular subject is fraught with inaccuracies—even glaring untruths. Get off the subject p.d.q.

HOW TO BECOME
A SUCCESSFUL BLUFFER

It's vital to accept that you can't be an accomplished bluffer in everything. There are subjects, such as brain surgery and skydiving (where the motto which begins "If at first you don't succeed" is of no practical use), which should be left to experts. We suggest you start by taking on one art, one sport, one social subject, and one leisure activity, and then purchasing the appropriate Bluffer's Guides. From these you can usually find a subject that your opponent takes pains to avoid. For instance, if he or she leads off with, "Did you see Carl Sagan's explanation of the 'Big Bang Theory' on PBS last night?" (and there is a better than average chance that you'll face some know-it-all who asks you a question like this), nip the query in the bud. Counter with, "I rarely watch television – I'm really into my computer (weight lifting, bonsai cuttings, registered shelties, stained glass, Bergman films, and so forth)."

If your opponent then shows signs of knowing something about computers (weight lifting, bonsai, shelties, stained glass, Bergman, and so forth) or turns out to be an IBM programmer who actually *knows* about computers *and* Bergman films, you need a well-prepared exit route, such as, "But, hey, computers should be used and not heard about, right?" Then adroitly switch to, "Have you seen the dates for the spring hot-air balloon rally?" Chances are, this may be your lucky break. But you have to have a grasp of the basics from the appropriate Bluffer's Guide. We aren't suggesting that these gambits have the makings of good conversation, only an escape from the vast wasteland of incomprehensibilia that constitute *his* home turf.

Method

The essential factor to master is *style,* and here's some classic methods:

The Question

Put most of your remarks in the form of questions, particularly when you're on the defensive and failing fast. Preface or terminate your most telling comments with the phrase "Don't you think . . . ?" This has a subtle element of conciliation about it.

The Hedge

Never commit yourself totally. Use phrases like "I'm inclined to think" and "Perhaps there's something to be said for . . ." You may then retract if you find you've gone too far in any one direction. The ultimate hedge is, of course,

The Look of Disbelief

The retreat of the bluffer is *silence,* but a firm, unflinching, disbelieving or cynical stare can lead to a major coup for you – particularly if you happen to be at a loss for words. Unfortunately, this device works only once per conversation.

Playing for Time

Less drastic, but highly effective. There's never any harm in murmuring, "I'll have to think it over." Even if, by some chance, you know what you're talking about, it's a reasonable request, one that no civilized person should refuse.

Interjection

This can range from a quiet "Mmm" to a surprised "Oh," an outraged "Mah Gawd!", a contemptuous snort, or a sardonic smirk. But by far the most effective is "Really?" in a questioning, even doubtful tone. This puts some people off their stride and goads others into a frenzy. The snort is an old, well-tried resort of the bluffer. It shouldn't be overdone lest you appear vulgar, but done right, almost imperceptibly, it's extremely effective. There's also the grunt, which is, in some ways, even better than the snort. Snorts tend to be hostile and disparaging; the grunt has an indefinite quality about it and might rattle your adversary.

Ambiguity

The whole essence of state-of-the-art bluffing is to make other people uncertain as to your exact meaning. This can be achieved by using such phrases as "I used to think," which leaves it open as to whether you still do or now don't.

Invention

This is perhaps the last resort of the resourceful bluffer, but it's nonetheless effective. To succeed, you have to sound convincing, and, if you yourself encounter this ploy with someone else, parry with equal enthusiasm. If someone says to you, "What do you think of Schwelschmann's *Zither Concerto in B Minor?*" (and you have reasonable doubts that Schwelschmann ever wrote anything for the zither, much less in a minor key), reply enthusiastically, "I prefer something more passionate – something like Kazimoto's *Mellophone Fantasia.*" Now *you* have the upper hand! Your adversary is trapped in his own invention.

Gesticulation

Anyone who has a natural knack for wild gestures has a useful weapon for diverting attention from the conversation at hand. The real art is to say one thing and gesticulate another. For example, while championing the cause of Freudian psychology in the twentieth century, continue shaking your head in disbelief. This ploy can throw even the most adroit of adversaries.

Dress

It might not seem important or even relevant to bluffing but **the right clothes** remain an integral part of the art. As P. T. Barnum maintained, no one can win an argument if he's wearing an orange Mae West life jacket with all the straps flapping in the breeze. Dressing for bluffing *is* important – an effective way to throw people off balance. Who'd believe a priest in a bow tie or a protest marcher in a Chanel jacket and gold chains? The practiced bluffer should learn the art of sartorial camouflage and use it to his own advantage. Eccentric getups only support the notion that bluffers are imposters.

Props

Hugh Hefner is a great champion of the pipe, and there's no doubt of its efficacy both as a time-waster and a way of choking your opponent past intelligible speech. Unfortunately, pipe smokers account for only 2.387 per cent of the male population (though possibly more among philosophers) and are almost negligible among women.

The more practical prop for the bluffer is the drink — whether alcoholic or not. Besides the obvious, distracting ways of sipping it, posturing with it, and running a finger around the rim, you can also distract a conversational opponent by offering to refill his glass or, in a real moment of crisis, refill your own.

Delivery

Try to adopt a slow, measured, and patient tone of voice, as if you knew what you were saying and had carefully thought it all out. This tactic will give the effect of self-confidence. Your subliminal message to your opponent is: I will *not* tolerate contradiction. Failing this, there are a number of equally helpful alternatives. The following are various standard gimmicks, drawn mainly from *60 Minutes* interviews, where bluffing approaches a fine art.

Sincere

Used by virtually all televangelists and burial plot salespeople. The normally demanding voice is made to sound smoothly unctuous. For a quick study, rerun video tapes of Barbara Walters interviewing Muammar Qaddafi.

Earnest or Serious

A technique used successfully by such figures as recently convicted stock manipulators and alleged Iran/Contra "heroes." People are easily fooled by this technique, but don't attempt to be simultaneously sincere *and* earnest or you'll wind up sounding and looking like an aging altar boy.

Smiling

Can be a fiasco, as demonstrated by former President Carter and Anita Bryant. For some reason, this is frequently adopted by people who have a lot of very white teeth. This ploy is especially disconcerting if used in conversations about the most recent air disaster or the state of the economy.

Offensive

(By *offensive,* we mean being *on* the offensive rather than *being* offensive, although the two are frequently linked). Fine-tuned by a master, Golda Meir, who affirmed that "The best defense is a good offense," this ruse is often used effectively by interviewers such as Sam Donaldson, and likewise by good divorce lawyers and recently canned NFL coaches. Basically, the idea is to intimidate the adversary.

Overwhelming

Practiced by Goldie Hawn and Carol Channing. Use so many words and nonsequiturs and deliver them at such a dizzying pace that your rivals soon find themselves outplayed. This ruse can be combined with a smile if you're Southern and female and accustomed to smiling and chattering simultaneously and can do so without dislocating your jaw.

Omniscient

Inevitably successful, but it *does* demand a fair amount of chutzpah and the right voice. The tone is confidential and controlled, such as Alistair Cooke's or William F. Buckley, Jr.'s. Nobody would dream of questioning what they say; their method is meant to disarm — and it works.

Cynical or Mocking

Used by people who're faking Old Money backgrounds. This is effective, but you can easily over-emphasize the bluffing content of what you're saying. It pays, if you're trying to sound cynical, to sound like Peter O'Toole or James Mason, both masters of the art.

Nice

Generally works well because people are less aggressive toward people who appear pleasant. Captain Kangaroo and most country singers cultivate niceness. The Vacant Look, used by Peter Sellers, Carol Burnett, and Pee Wee Herman, has much the same effect. It puts people off-guard — almost immediately

Innocent at Large

Usefully employed by Doris Day, Gomer Pyle, and June Cleaver. A winner every time. If you don't believe it, read the reviews of the latest Walt Disney release.

Eccentric

Fairly successful, at least as a *temporary* diversion. Use facial tics, hurried or impaired speech, and an accent. All of these have been stock-in-trade for such notable stand-up comedians as Lily Tomlin, Red Skelton, Jackie Gleason, Bill Cosby, and Robin Williams. For an in-depth case study, review all Meryl Streep roles until you have it mastered.

Bluff

Probably the best. The user pretends to be a good, honest soul, just like you and me. The supreme master of the bluff approach is former President Reagan, who got himself elected and re-elected by this simple, but effective, fool-proof method.

GOOD BLUFFING SUBJECTS

The Arts

The arts have always provided a bounty of good bluffing material. Even if you're only in a casual conversation, eventually you'll find yourself at odds with the tastes of a fellow listener, reader, or museum-goer. It's just a matter of time.

Music

Outside of the "academies" (possibly inside them as well), nobody actually *talks* about the science of music—that is, downbeats, harmonics, and technical stuff. Or even about a specific piece of music. Can you imagine two average people comparing Beethoven's First and Second Symphonies? Neither can we. So if someone touches upon Beethoven, you discuss so-and-so's *performance* of any given Beethoven symphony and the *appalling* mess he made of it. Now *that* you can get your teeth into. Anyone watching or listening to a symphony (or even a cassette of a Beethoven symphony) can remark with complete confidence that the orchestra was "under-rehearsed" and "unwillingly following the conductor's tempo," or "lacking in understanding." If you're watching the performance on TV, remember that all the performers are natural bluffers—

especially during close-ups. They probably wish they were home watching late-night talk shows or old Bette Davis movies.

It's fortunate that classical music, as a *living* art, has died out—for the most part. Nowadays, the major portion of the public (and most performers) are interested only in music of the past. Only a fraction would attend a program of **modern music**, and most of those only because a noted director is involved—such as Zubin Mehta, the musical matrons' heartthrob. There's not much point, therefore, in a musical bluffer doing *lots* of research on contemporary music since few people, including experts, are likely to discuss it.

If you want to bone up on composers, the only thing you really need to have up your sleeve are the names of the least known and least liked works—such as Scarlatti's *Piano Concerto in G* or Prokofiev's dirges. Trot these names out with boring regularity and insist that they are sadly neglected and underrated because the public hasn't been properly trained to appreciate them. For a stunning trump, add that Scarlatti is an *acquired* taste, appealing to only the most *sensitive* ear.

Remember, too, that not all music is classical. You can score heavily in any company by a superficial knowledge of **jazz** or, better yet, some specialized area of jazz, like **ragtime** or **swing**. Jazz introduced a new language to music. It was no longer something that you could write down in a simple, translatable form and then play in a correct manner, like "Buffalo Gals" or "The Minute Waltz." It was improvised in a noisy and belligerent, sometimes wantonly sensual style. In this guise, jazz evolved into the basis of all popular music since the 1920s, especially the music known as **pop.**

There are two main divisions of jazz: **traditional** — the earlier form with a tune, and **modern** — the current kind without a tune, which wanders on like a ranting drunken uncle with a foreign brogue until it collapses in a noisy, jangling heap. Jazz offers several possible topics to the feisty bluffer. To bop or *not* to bop — that is a worthy question. To enhance your pseudo-expertise, you should refer to boppers and non-boppers by name. You can invent any number of jazz musicians with strange names. For openers, try Lancelot Link or Etta Place. There are so many *real* odd ones that no one will notice the difference.

Jazz is a sort of **folk music** which wasn't written by anybody, but it's played by almost everybody — whether musical or not — and most of them aren't. It's always slightly off-key or out of sync. According to one critic, you can always tell genuine folk singers from phony ones by the way they cup an ear with a hand and sing through their noses, thus leaving their mouths free for a swig of booze or a shared joint. Most folk singers come from Nashville or the Blue Ridge Mountains of West Virginia. Most of them leave their humble origins as soon as the money is right and set up housekeeping on less humble premises, often with a young, well-endowed devotee, soon to be replaced by serial clones.

As for pop: first of all there was **rock 'n' roll** which was boogie-woogie with blues-type lyrics added. Then there was **rhythm 'n' blues** (all pop singers say 'n'), which was blues with a touch of boogie-woogie. After this, pop (including soft rock, hard rock, and hard metal rock) seems to be all you ever hear on the radio, going on 'n' on 'n' on. Finally, it killed off the art of musical criticism.

Pop groups proliferate at the rate of approximately 15 per day. Pop is incredibly popular and some people wear Walkmans all the time so they won't miss a single note. Walkmans make it difficult to indulge in any sort of normal conversation, let alone a chance to bluff.

Opera

This is a field where the bluffer should step warily, as *all* opera fanatics are quirky and potentially volatile. To begin with, they seem to be able to lose themselves in hours of yowling melodrama. They have, in fact, gone into a deep trance, like sloths or meditation freaks. This is true. Listen to their other-worldly conversations. It's the kind you'd find when conversing with Tibetan monks and dedicated astrologers.

Opera poses several problems. If you really *like* music, you're unlikely to want to have it spoiled by a lot of amateur actors wandering around the stage in outlandish costumes. If, on the other hand, you like acting, you wouldn't choose to go to the opera for similar reasons, even though opera plots are notoriously great theater, having sprung from street performances that resembled modern soap operas.

The basic plot of nine out of ten operas concerns a hero or heroine (or both) who live in a state of confusion, not realizing that their lover is faithful though they appear not to be, or not recognizing them at all because they're wearing a mask or a helmet with horns. At the end of the opera, they die of

(1) a high note they couldn't *quite* reach – resulting in a ruptured diaphragm
(2) inexplicable grief
(3) T.B.

(4) suicide

(5) a combination of any and all of 1 through 5.

In order to be an opera bluffer, you should listen to *recorded* opera (don't even *think* of sitting through a 3-hour live performance), but this method, like most things, has its drawbacks. Because of the strain of having to set all those words to music, composers come up with, on the average, only one hummable tune per opera. The better ones might have more—possibly two or three. Buy only cassettes or CD's of opera "highlights." Another bluffer's trick is to revere the golden voices of the past. This provides a possible dodge because many people may not be that familiar with Emma Eames or Bidú Sayaö.

Remember, no serious opera should ever be taken seriously, just as no comic opera should be laughed at. The most treacherous waters for the beginning opera bluffer is Wagner, a very specialized taste. The bluffer is advised to steer clear of anything that smacks of Norse folklore or requires a crane to lift the diva's costume—or the diva herself, for that matter.

Theater

There are several good reasons for going to the theater, but most people go for the same reason: so that they can say that they "have been to the theater." It never hurts to smile knowingly when a fellow playgoer mentions a certain "star." A small smirk and smaller praise lets your opponent know that you're on to the "star game" and don't intend to kowtow to public opinion, no matter how entrenched the star system. An obscure comment on the potential of a minor actor—for example, the ingenue who played the *au pair* girl, might lead your opponent to believe that you can spot real talent.

Other ways to disguise that fact that theater-going is not your forte is to praise the set designer, an otherwise unsung individual. Note how the colors of the drapes, the upholstery, and the costumes all enhance one another *and* the "emotional dimension" of the second act. Spike your commentary with a snide remark ("Critics have *always* found the dialogue in that act too meager to stand alone."). This calls for just the right interpretive gesture. Then sip *Perrier avec citron* and wait for someone to challenge the astuteness of your observation.

Art

The fine arts were born of bluffery. Most people only see what they *think* they see. They're susceptible therefore to being persuaded that what they *think* they see is not what they *ought* to see. Or what they *ought* to see is what some bluffer or other *thinks* they *ought* to see. It's the ideal field to be in.

If you're standing in front of a large canvas which is entirely black except for a small orange spatter in one corner, and the expert says "How profound," agree. The artist may have titled this masterpiece, which is being offered at a mere $75,000, "Thoughts Before Conception." Why even bother to disagree with that? Likewise, when you come across a small pile of pebbles labeled "United Nations," or a zit-cratered rock with a hole in the middle called "Gwen," don't be daunted. As quickly as possible, get yourself into *real* art, the older sort of thing, where words like *arrangement*, perspective, depth, intransigence, balance, and *balderdash* are all yours for the asking.

In the field of modern art, use a more modern vocabulary—*obvious, viable, amplitude*, and so on. Once you get into the swing of it, your bluff is as good as anyone else's. If you're really feeling up to it, go for two-word comments, such as *surrealistic drive, subjective karma*, or *latter-day anathema*. Then your opponent has twice as much to de-bluff before coming up with what he hopes is a suitably clever comeback. By that time, you'll have wandered amiably on toward the next abstract horror.

Literature

Unlike music and art, literature can be interpreted by most people. It's simply a matter of reading. As a result, most people think they know something about it, and lots of them even write it. Surprisingly, some of the least proficient semi-talents make the most money—Jacqueline Susann, Norman Mailer, Tom Wolfe, and Harold Robbins. But their technique—self-promotion—comes under a different set of bluffer's rules. (See Business)

Preeminent in literature is Shakespeare, who wrote an enormous amount. Certain plays of his are known to everyone because they're so full of quotations. He invented a sort of linguistic affectation that makes complete nonsense sound very profound: for example, "Ann hath a way with her that doth nip the portals of my soul like the pincers of a half-baked lobster." That sort of thing has been fertile grounds for interpretation and scholarly inquiry ever since. This is why, however much you feel like snorting, you should treat the name of Shakespeare with the utmost reverence. Some people even rank Shakespeare with God and say they don't believe he existed at all.

After Shakespeare come all the classics. These were written by writers whom no one actually reads—except when they have to. Names like Chaucer, Milton, Melville, Hawthorne, and Spenser—particularly Spenser. A line or two learned from somewhere deep in the latter portion of one of their longer works, where no man has ever trod, will prove beyond any doubt that you're no fool when it comes to literature. (Keep your *Bartlett's* close at hand.)

Rating only slightly below these are the "readable classics." These are the ones that most people have read a chapter or two of (or seen the movie)—like works by Dickens and Kipling, Hemingway and Steinbeck. Generally they're from a later period and therefore more linguistically accessible. The thing here is not to go for the obvious—like *Oliver Twist* or *The Grapes of Wrath*, both of which have been filmed—but to read a chapter (no need to go farther than that) of *Hard Times* or *The Wayward Bus*.

The rest of literature can then be rated according to its readability. Top marks go to those who are virtually unreadable—James Joyce or William Faulkner; at the bottom are those who are readily understandable, particularly if the authors toss in good-sized chunks of whimsy or humor, like Mark Twain and Ray Bradbury do. But you'll score more points if you stick to the dull and unwieldy. After all, anybody can read *Huckleberry Finn*.

People who have become blatantly popular, like Ian Fleming, Agatha Christie, Mickey Spillane, or Florence

King, can now be discussed as you would folk art or "cult art" and given some status (but not too much) in this new critical era.

Business

There exist areas of human endeavor where the whole structure of social conduct and working relationships depends on the art of bluffery—not applied with malice, but simply as a means of self-preservation. The business world is a prime example: it's founded entirely on bluff.

Business, by its very nature, requires a knack for bamboozling both colleague and competitor into a belief that you know what you're doing and can be trusted. Anyone in business will recognize the difficulty of this maneuver for those would-be entrepreneurs who are

(1) blatantly inept,
(2) corrupt enough to sell sour popsicles to the Pope, or
(3) employed by a company that is both inept and corrupt.

The bamboozler, if relationships are to survive and business be transacted, must make a sincere effort to get away with it. The only way to best him is to build a well-balanced bastion of bluff.

Business splits itself into various ill-defined areas of activity, one of which you should choose as your main bluffing stronghold, with a fringe bluffing knowledge of all the others, most of which you'll have to cope with at some time or other. The crucial areas are these:

Accounting

The art of proving, by some means or other, that the books balance, the business is solvent, too much tax is being paid, and you are worthy of your hire. Not necessarily in that order.

Advertising

The art of convincing everyone that, because you know the game and can be trusted, they'd do well to buy from you.

Computers

The justification for substantial reductions in traditional staff in order to employ additional staff to cope with all the extra work that is caused by supplanting fallible employees with fallible machines. (See Data Processing.)

Finance

The practical way of convincing everyone that you know the game, can be trusted, *and* can make a profit out of it, in spite of vicious lies or, at best, questionable exaggerations being spread by the company accountant.

Management

The art of proving to those who work under you that you know the game. There's no point trying to convince people in management that you're trustworthy. They wouldn't recognize trustworthiness in a field of two.

Marketing

The art of getting what you sell to the people who want to buy it. Success in this area just may convince them of your competence. If not, there's always sales, the last resort of the inept and the corrupt.

Public Relations

The art of convincing everyone that you can be trusted—in spite of the fact that you clearly don't know diddly-squat about business.

Quality Control

Setting standards and producing; for example, making sure that your company makes duct tape that really sticks, balls that really bounce, and curling irons that don't fry hair forms a major part of this department's business. If carrying a clipboard and making little checkmarks in the appropriate boxes has any allure for you, then this is your bailiwick. If not, shop for better nesting grounds.

Research and Development

The *pièce de résistence* of bluffery! Only the most accomplished fakery can get you a place in this creative wing of the business establishment. After you snag a post, it's up to you to make up potential products and suggest ways that they can be manufactured. How they get sold is somebody else's headache. (See Marketing.)

Salesmanship

Proving that, although you probably can't be trusted, you *do* know how to turn a fast buck. But only if no one asks too many questions about your products and methods. Especially methods.

Data Processing

Top drawer bluffers can sail through most subjects, but they may face sudden death if the talk suddenly veers toward **computers**, an unavoidable topic in this day of hardware (the mainframe type, not deadbolt locks, saws, hammers, and plumbers helpers.)

The main line of defense here is to hang out with people over forty, very few of whom have delved any further than you have into the occult world of data processing. *Never* broach the subject to a child. Children under fifteen converse naturally on the subject, prattling on about pixels, baud rates, external disk drives, and joysticks. (All of which sound remotely titillating, but they arrived in the kids' Christmas stockings, so how risqué can they be?)

The other group to avoid are **computer experts**; however, they're by no means invulnerable, since a few *are* over forty. Like most experts, they can be baffled by simple, straightforward questions, and, because few of them have any sense of humor (at least the normal variety), they are easily thrown off by flippancy. Remark that, in general, computer whizzes lack social skills, because they spend long hours in dimly lit cubicles talking to themselves and caressing keyboards, floppies, and their mouse. Marshal all your forces toward group discussion in order to capitalize on their inability to carry on normal human conversation.

To succeed, you won't need skill with computers as much as a path through the language maze. At present, a reasonably intelligent person can read the whole data processing section of *Consumer Reports,* or any computer magazine or manual (the latter usually translated from Japanese by a Czechoslovakian) without understanding a single word of it. The entire computer world is so peppered with names, jargon, and acronyms (for example, WYSIWYG, DOS, Kermit, FIDO, Lotus, Red Rider, GIGO, Savior, and so forth) that the weak, desperate ruse of inventing a few more can be highly successful.

Should you, by a stroke of the good fairy's wand, come up against uncertain bluffers in the computer field, dismiss their tentative inaccuracies with a groan, exasperatedly sighing, "Not *another* boring Z-80 crate!" Then launch aggressively into a heartless attack on their claims by comparing their outmoded Atari (Mac, Lisa, Commodore, IBM compatible, *ad nauseam*) with your new Aristotle, "The New Age Cerebrum."

Before your victim has time to cast doubts on the Aristotle's validity (which they can hardly do, if you maintain that you own the definitive, state-of-the-art model), you should move on to greener and less-grazed pastures, such as the Aristotle's speed, interface capacity, and anti-viral device. You should also add obliquely that the Aristotle uses the new interlinear, intercapacitor chips as well as a full range of voice command pull-down menus *and* synthesizer.

None of the old 64K RAMs for you! Only the 1 Meg BUMs which link up with the micro-Bollox business system *and* feature external ports for modem, CD, fax, and a color laser copier. Plus, they require the Even-Softa software. (At this point, your voice trails off. You could go on, but the others will, by now, seem a bit boggled.) As a final fillip, add that your machine is not bothered by mice, a problem that has oppressed hackers since the Apple first steamrolled UNIVAC. It's no wonder that former programmers suffered with rodents plaguing their fruit bowl.

There's a danger, however, that, by this time, your adversary may have realized that you're a raving loony. If you sense that he's about to aim a zinger at you on behalf of his Atari—which could be boring well beyond the Z-80 mark—quickly make it clear that you have lost all interest in the subject. Casually inject a newsy tidbit such as, "I understand that Steven Jobs has sent out specs on a revolutionary laptop that not only prints, but collates, staples, and inserts into envelopes as well." Then beat a hasty retreat to the john.

Business Correspondence

The business bluffer reaches nirvana in interoffice memos and business letters. After muddling up the reader's attention with such arcane terms as *re, pursuant to, cognizant of, in compliance with*, and *as per*, the bluffer can bury the basic idea of the text so deeply that the reader will never get it. This skill with businessese will so baffle and impress any reader that he will assume that the content was well worth the effort. (Note: one should add *she* these days, since women have followed men up the circuitous goat paths of entrepreneurship—a word invented years ago in order to impress wives and laymen, and has now almost entirely replaced the simpler term, "business.")

The Boardroom

Boardroom tactics, among the finest of bluffdom's three levels (return to **Scoring** if you haven't been paying enough attention to remember!), require a number of razor-sharp prerequisites. Most obviously, the board-room tactician must dress the part: gray suit, impeccably shined wingtips (medium-high heels for women), low-gloss dress shirt with circumspect monogram (no more than ⅝" high and *always* white-on-white), predominently red or blue silk tie (depending upon the scope and depth of your presentation; save paisleys for interviews and reindeer for the office Christmas party), no-nonsense horn-rims (wire rims went out with Haight-Ashbury and the Jefferson Airplane), and a low-key leather portfolio – never a fold-out briefcase with a date-minder, a dead giveaway of the rookie.

Other adjuncts to an impressive performance before the CEO and other notables of the business world include the following:

Easel

Buttress the most meaningless statistics with flow charts, pie charts, bar graphs, and overlays of the most obtuse types and styles. Since computers now draw and color these for you, you don't have to spend hours with felt tip markers, compass, and T-square. (See Data Processing)

Pointer

To bluff with finesse, point abstractedly up and down the planes of your flow charts. If you catch a wary fellow bluffer giving you the great hairy eyeball, aim your pointer straight ahead and **P**unch **O**ut **Y**our **W**ords for maximum effect. Use a subliminal suggestion of succinctness and skill by purchasing a tele-scoping pointer, which you deftly *snap!* into the palm of your hand at the climactic moment.

Handouts

Distribute various sheets of data *throughout* your presentation rather than at the beginning. This diversionary method keeps the guy on the end wondering when the stack will get to him and whether he'll actually receive the last copy or will have to share with the person to his left. (For greater effectiveness, photocopy extremely erudite source material, whether it suits the topic or not. Try *College English, AMA Journal,* or *Psychological Abstracts* for the least readable material. Or use your imagination. There's plenty of bluffery in the publishing world.)

Name-dropping

It's an old, established method of scoring points. Nothing has replaced good old-fashioned name-dropping as a means of impressing. If you aren't up on the people who are in the most recent headlines (for example, Trump, Merv Griffin, Iacocca), fall back on masters of the past, such as J. P. Morgan, John Jacob Astor, or one of the early Rockefellers. For an even greater wallop, quote a line or two from Keynes; for example, "In the long run we are all dead."

Jargon

Like business correspondence and computers, board-room talk centers on the proper repetition of certain mantras—that is, language which indicates that you're *in* with the in-crowd. The more successful phrases and terms include *state-of-the-art, net-net,* and *bottom line.* But you can often fall back on seasoned terminology, such as *s.o.p., a.s.a.p.,* and *"have your girl get in touch with my girl."* (This last has been thoroughly trounced by the women's movement, but in select conservative businesses, such as old-line investment firms, women still receive little more than a cursory tip of the hat, even though they probably run the whole show for minimum wage.)

Cards and Games

If you indulge in cards of any kind, you have to be a serious bluffer. Starting with poker (as cited in our introductory pages), most card games embody the art of bluffing translated into visual reality. There's virtually no card game (with the possible exception of Old Maid) that isn't based on making your opponent believe that you possess something which you don't. This is true of poker, bridge, canasta, pinochle, Uno, Rook, gin rummy, and Go Fish and constitutes what bluffing is all about. In fact, a working knowledge of card games is an essential asset to The Compleat Bluffer.

Board games are a little trickier. These include Monopoly, chess, backgammon, Chinese checkers, and particularly Scrabble, a game which has more rabid aficionados than Radio Shack junkies or Volvo owners. Whatever the board game, bluffing requires *some* knowledge of the game. To extricate yourself from a ticklish situation, such as placing a hotel on the Reading Railroad, forming the plural of *zeugma,* or checkmating a bishop, immediately apologize for misleading your opponent and ask, "Are you following the standard rules — or the rules of the *newer* game, which were invented to challenge fifth-level players?"

Pool requires a more studied grace. After failing to establish yourself as a champeen hustler, retreat into nit-picking. Question anything — the lighting, the table balance, the straightness of the cues, and the weight of the balls. When all else fails, notice a hairline fracture or a minuscule knick in the eight ball and place your cue on the table in disgust. Finally, complain that you were just looking forward to some *real* competition, since you've recently been barred from amateur play-offs.

Country Club Sports

It's in country club sports that bluffing moves into the social realm. The thing here, of course, is that belonging to a club is of far greater significance than the sport (or sports) around which the club revolves. Members inhabit a world of blazers and ties, receptions and committees, greens privileges and locker assignments, social status and admission to the bar only in proper dress. Women, too, get swept up in the social whirl of member-guest tournaments, but the basic club player is the young boy wonder of the financial world, out to best his yuppie competitor on the racquetball court.

The same expectations apply to most clubs. Tennis and golf are comparatively friendly examples where the pecking order can be bent slightly on the strength of a drink or two. This variance from earlier generations of clubgoers results from the fact that Americans have grown tired of both tennis and golf and don't take them as seriously as aerobics or jogging—pastimes which have become so important that they are practically religions now. A wise bluffer might well deem it wise to specialize in them alone.

Aerobics

It's important to remember that aerobics was once a dull and dreary activity known as calisthenics, which reached its height as a means of torture for Marine recruits at Parris Island. Couched in strictly macho terms—jumping jacks and squat-thrusts—calisthenics once suited the male need to flex muscles, sweat, and work off aggressions. It also gave ample excuses to grunt, puff, and confirm Darwin's theories about early men dragging women around by the hair of the head or beating a hairy chest with a beefy fist.

Gradually, women, duped into believing they could replace a middle-age spread with a Scarlett O'Hara waistline, took over the field and added a new twist to an old game: physical fitness for the sake of the heart—and any other organ that requires toning. Now, instead of seeing recruits slogging ruggedly through the rain to the cadence of group recitations of scurrilous military doggerel, the eye falls upon women of all ages, sizes, shapes, and conditions as they bend, flex, bump, and grind to the sound of the Pointer Sisters while gazing at the gyrations of their flexotard-clad abs and glutes in floor-to-ceiling mirrors.

To legitimize the expense for *haute couture* athletic shoes and togs, coordinated leg warmers, and zippered carry-alls, aerobics fans pause at appropriate moments and check their active heartrates against at-rest lub-dubs. If the gain is worth mentioning, they compare notes with other pulse-takers, who knowingly intone the mantra "No pain, no gain." All smile in mutual martyrdom and chug back into formation, executing hip roll-outs simultaneously with arm curls and neck rotations.

Conversational bluffing on the subject of aerobics is based almost entirely based on knowledge gleaned from TV warm-ups or Jane Fonda tapes, although anybody who was anybody is making a comeback these days with warm-up tapes of his/her own—from Richard Simmons to Angela Lansbury. To achieve any status with those in the know, one has to be able to say, without hesitation, how much the game has improved since low-impact has taken the place of that god-awful method that began the rush to muscledom. Or how much better shock-absorbing running shoes assist the body in reaching the "max of cardiovascular output."

Depending on your age or physical condition, you might want to think about touting stretching exercises, which are safer for those over forty or people whose backs have already rejected the rigors of high-speed pelvic thrusts set to heavy metal rock. To establish your place as a savant, lean back against the nearest Jacuzzi jet and invent a few facts and figures connecting the bouncy approach with osteoporosis, cartilage damage, or whatever degenerative disease holds current sway with the glitterati, and you're a shoo-in. But don't try too hard to impress. You might find yourself demonstrating for a gathering and trying to explain why your sacro suddenly disengaged your iliac.

Fitness

Being fit has become such a mania with modern society that you have to take a positive attitude toward it. It's no use being half and half. Either you declare that you're dedicated to keeping fit – in which case you have a great deal of bluffing to do, as only ten percent of the population are fully fit, and most of those are younger than 25. *Or* you declare that you've "never had a day's illness," a comment that will infuriate most people beyond coherence – particularly if it happens to be true, but of course truth is *not* of the the utmost in these situations.

When pushed to the limit by a real body buff, retreat into bluffing your way through **nutrition,** which is anybody's game these days. Disclose the fact that you have to give up fast accelerations of heart rate until your polyunsaturated glycerides level off or your intake of roughage depletes the build-up of cholesterol in your spleen. Then rifle your pockets for a pill (a lint ball will do) which proves that you are serious about matters of health – to the point of hourly mineral toners to ward off inhaled pollutants. For a stunning show-stopper, raise one eyebrow and assert that, according to the Surgeon General, the celery water fast may someday replace the triple bypass.

The average person has something wrong some-where most of the time. It's therefore even more ef-fective if you can link your robust health with the "don't-care" attitude and claim that, like a relative of yours who lived to be over a hundred, you believe in "eating, drinking, and smoking to excess" as the recipe for a long and active life. Otherwise, as Twain warned, you won't have any excess baggage to throw overboard and will die from neglecting your habits.

Jock Sports

In the realm of TV jock sports (football, basketball, baseball, golf), you're on safer bluffing turf. From the distance of your nose to the TV screen, you can fake any number of impressive stances about the qualifications of the latest "hot properties," especially those players whose private lives leave questions about ethical training. If, for example, an astounding drop kick leaves your fellow sports fans breathless with admiration, you can shift the spotlight to yourself with a *sotto voce* remark about steroids clogging the pores of young athletes and leaving them too pockmarked for Wheaties commercials. Remind the guys, too, that steroids shrivel up the testicles to the size of a pea.

During long runs of Olympic footage, try to maintain the image of a purveyor of *all* sports by commenting on how young viers for Olympic medals have sullied the original spirit of the games by concerning themselves too heavily with politics and endorsements for foot powder and diet cola. Then shift rapidly to an intense analysis of the intricacies of sportscasting before anyone asks for particulars. To make your point, require absolute silence until the next figure skater, diver, triathlete, slalomer, luger, or what have you completes the course. Then fall back on the bluffer's favorite ploy, "Hey, how about that camera angle?"

Leisure and Hobbies

When a person steps away from a vocation and into the fantasy world of an avocation or a hobby, some really potent bluffing comes into action. Even if his or her employment is the lowliest and least cerebral, everyone becomes an expert—or, more politely, an enthusiast—in the hobby racket. Be it miniature vegetable growing, iceboating, cross-country skiing, Sicilian wines, or netsuke collecting—wise bluffers should either beware of becoming entangled with an enthusiast or else prepare themselves by way of the appropriate Bluffer's Guide.

Enthusiasts are so obsessed with their obsessions that they have little time for anything else. Whereas the more generalized bluffer will ease into a conversation with some inane twaddle about the weather, traffic, or the current bear market, the specialized enthusiast will plunge right in with a leading remark, such as "Do you garden?" or "Didn't I see you down at the rifle range last weekend?" or "Seen any grosbeaks this spring?" or "Have you tried the latest Cuisinart blade for slicing shiitake?" The bluffer's best answers, in order, are "No"; "Me? I've been too absorbed dividing rhizomes"; "No grosbeaks—but I did see several *flamingos plastique*"; and "We've spent most of our weekends stone-grinding our own oat bran." If all else fails to deflate the enthusiast from an obsession, duck out at the first available moment or develop a sneezing fit and claim that allergies have been *deva*sting because of the unseasonably wet (dry) weather. If you happen to have read the appropriate Bluffer's Guide, of course, stand your ground—whatever the challenge.

Do-It-Yourselfers

A popular area for home bluffing is **Do-It-Yourself** (DIY) projects. There are basically two kinds of DIYers: those who *can* and those who *buy books* on the subject. This rule applies to everything from laying brick sidewalks or hanging a windsock to building a redwood deck around the homemade lily pond.

Inept DIYers are a pathetic bunch, huddled together beside long rows of gleaming bandsaws and routers that have never been in operation and passing around cold beers of consolation. They take to DIY either because they fantasize they are among the can-doers — in which case you're called upon to admire crooked shelving, botched attempts at hanging wallpaper, and home-installed quadraphonic systems — or because they defy the **Get Someone Else To Do It For You** mind-set (or GSETDIFY). As for you, try to pretend (bluff) that the shelves, wallpaper, and woofers and tweeters are *terrific* ("looks like a professional did it"). Eventually even your DIYer will detect that the bookshelves list badly to port, lilies and stems fail to match on the wallpaper, and the sound system has a drumbeat like a pacemaker on speed. But you could be fooled here, since plenty of married DIYers are capable of bluffing themselves until they practically kill themselves DIYing. These DIYers are impossible. They will try to coax superlatives from you over what they have just DIYed. "But it must have cost thousands!" they expect you to murmur. "No, we did it *ourselves*" comes the immodest answer. "And in only seven weekends, not counting the Saturday night and Sunday morning my honey spent at County General having a steel splinter removed from her medulla oblongata."

It's your *duty* to deflate DIYers, whether good *or* bad. If they're good, they're unbearable; if they're bad, they present a hazard to life and limb. When shown a newly installed sauna, don't hesitate to rap sharply on the frame and warn, "But this doesn't come up to Consumer's Union specs." Poke or pull anything you can (under the guise of looking out for the DIYer's personal safety). If it comes off or collapses, you're in a strong position. After you've detached a few drawer handles and ripped out a switch or two, the DIYer will begin to lose confidence. If you're a bad DIYer yourself, make sure that your own recent lines of demarcation are well covered by strategically placed house plants.

GSETDIFY

The confirmed **GSETDIFY** is, on the other hand, either rich or bred-in-the-bone lazy. This sort of man would marry a woman with six children to save himself the effort. The female version would corrode at the notion of buffing her own nails and cringe at the thought of plugging in her own curling iron, except under the direst of circumstances (say, if she were on safari in Kenya — and remembered to bring the appropriate adapter.)

The GSETDIFYer is often more unbearable than the DIYer. A lightly dropped remark, such as "I simply asked the caterers to handle the whole show" is enough to make one drop all ties with the Republican party on the spot. Other equally abrasive comments include "Heavens, I don't even own an ironing board" or "Call the airlines? Whatever are travel agents for!"

However, even the GSETDIFYer suffers a bit while the project is in progress. Everyone has heard about the electrician who tears up the floorboards only to find out that it's the wrong room, the telephone installer who accidentally cuts into the TV cable, and the tree trimmer who makes work for his brother-in-law, the roofer.

The bluffing interplay is at its most virulent in these areas. Faced with a DIYer, one immediately assumes the mantle of a condescending GSETDIFYer; faced with a smug GSETDIFYer, one becomes an arrogant DIYer. Some ready phrases to use are: "You don't mean to say you *paid* to have that done!"; "Inlaid work seems so showy in these days of informal entertaining"; "Did you know you can get the same thing in plastic these days that looks just like intaglio?"; "How do you find the time? We're so rarely home during the summer — all that sticky heat, you know"; and "Do you intend to finish it sometime — or just leave it *au naturel?*"

Sex

Bluffing areas under the heading of sex fall mainly under the headings of Expectations, Titillation, and Waiting at the Church. It's in these areas that the art of the bluffer is most profitably expended. It can be so effectively deployed that successful bluffers earn a reputation without actually getting down to it at all. That is, if they want it that way. Or any of the other ways, of which there are so many.

Talking about sex seems almost as satisfying as the real thing — and not half so risky. Everyone, short of nuns and monks, is on an equal footing in the art of sex bluffing. Come to think about it — even monks and nuns. In fact, *especially* monks and nuns. And don't forget the elderly ladies at bridge club and the elderly old codgers playing horseshoes.

As with most subjects that we've touched on, there seems to be just two schools of thought on the matter of sex as an adjunct to life. You either believe, like most film directors, that sex is everything— the prime motive for living—or you believe that all that long, involved, tiring, expensive business of seduction seems hardly worth the brief (7 minutes max) end result. Sex dominates one of those great gray areas where you are never *quite* sure who is being bluffed—the doer or the doee. Assuming that you belong, as most people do, outside the pale of bluffery, but you feel the need to impress somebody who you think might be impressionable, these are some good lines to lob:

(1) You first tried to have sex with your twin at the age of six months, but your stroller tipped over;
(2) You first thought of having a serious affair at the age of twelve but opted for a *menage à cinq*;
(3) Your first sex partner was impressed, but not impressive;
(4) You can take it or leave it.

Languages

Surmounting language barriers requires an extremely skilled application of the bluffer's art. From early history on, the first tourists were usually uninvited and heavily armed. The Roman legionnaire trying to befriend the early Britons would say something like, "Ohum, quellum magnum dayum." The indignant native, assuming that the soldier was making fast and

loose with his daughter would reply, "Make tracks, dogmeat," leaving the Roman to figure out what he had said wrong. Failing to establish diplomatic ties, the dejected legionnaire went sadly on his way, raping and pillaging to pass the time and assuage his heavy heart.

As every tourist knows, the principle way to communicate with foreigners is to treat them as if they were deaf and daft and to shout sentences straight out of Tarzan movies, occasionally throwing in an "o" at the end of principal nouns, as in "Where is banco?" or "Me hungry. Me want food." The only truly foolproof way to bluff anybody into believing that you know a language is to greet the native in his or her own tongue with the equivalent of "Hi," for courtesy's sake. Then, to cover your tracks, declare yourself one of the following:

- Dutch, if in France
- Swedish, in all Mediterranean haunts
- Lithuanian everywhere else

Then in broken, halting English, suggest using English to communicate.

Politics

Politics ranks as the supreme subject for bluffing, mainly because it's 99.9% bluff in the first place. Nobody actually believes in politics, least of all those involved in it. The whole point of talking politics and inevitably revealing your political opinions is not to gain admiration for your firm convictions or even to promote them, but to establish your character, position, and degree of success.

Republicans, for instance, have a lot going for them: big bucks, the backing of the horsey set, and best of all, no actual policies to pursue beyond a belief that those who have, keep, and those who haven't: Keep Out. Thus, the purpose of right-wing bluffing is to put up a good pretense of caring for the state of the economy without actually thumbing your nose at the have-nots. This stance leaves the impression that you truly belong among the haves, even if your balance sheet suggests Chapter 11.

The **Democratic** political line is more difficult to maintain among certain circles because it involves definite policies based on dislike and envy. But the bluffer can profit from the assumption that voting as a left-winger marks one as more intelligent, philosophical, and more caring than the average person. It also provides a wider array of bumper stickers to choose from.

The best bluffing opportunities exist for the middle-of-the-roaders. These fence-sitters can profess both social conscience and vague leanings toward the left while living in posh neighborhoods, complete with hot tub, double garage, and children in snooty private schools. Most genuine bluffers belong to this twilight zone of the uncommitted, where they can argue both ways or straight up the middle. The whole basis of political argument is that, faced with a diehard rightist, you have to take a stance well to the left. For a staunch leftist, you reverse flags. With care, you still end up astride the fence with your political savvy intact, showing assiduous caution toward splinter groups.

Don't be misled into thinking that political argument has any influence on political thought. Those who don't know and don't think may switch allegiances according to what pollsters are saying, but real politicos are unchangeable. A few offbeat souls upset the generally acceptable pattern by actually believing in something, but this frail .1% aren't bluffing. If you meet such an animal, edge off crabwise and relocate in more fertile waters.

In political circles, you should be wary of appearances. The man in the pin-striped suit who gives every appearance of being a Yalie may well turn out to carry a banner for the left. Likewise, the impoverished spinster with the mismatched luggage may indeed hold blue chip stock and call the shots for an oil cartel. Political bluffing is calculated bluffing at its best, and you may find here an adversary worthy of your best efforts.

Class

There is no arena of in-fighting where bluffing is more necessary or beneficial than class warfare. Start by ignoring all attempts to convince yourself that class died out with the '38 Packard and that you're just a garden variety snob. Class is a lifeline, even though people have used it at times to hang themselves. Without class, a person wouldn't know what station in life to get off at, be it upper-upper-middle, lower-upper-middle, or Penn Central.

One does *not* discuss class in bluffing circles; you use it as a foil. First, size up what class your adversary belongs to. If you win that round, you're sitting in the catbird seat, ready to pounce. Of course, sizing up class isn't easy: class-sizing demands study. Even a Kentucky blueblood can have bad breath and five o'clock shadow or drive a pickup truck. And there's many an Alabama belle who overtipples on mint juleps and misuses her sorbet spoon and/or fish knife. Attitudes toward class change. Only noticeably every hundred years or so — but they change.

Up to about 1930, **blue collars** were considered either comical, criminal, or half-witted — or all three — and were thus portrayed in books, plays, and paintings. In the age of enlightenment that followed, farm laborers and mill workers demonstrated that they could be a nuisance as well — and had the votes to prove it. In song and movie, unions exalted the common man to the level of myth, leading the rest of society to wonder just who *does* have a right to sing the blues?

At the other extreme of myth, the silver-spooned **upper crust** are reputedly inclined toward sedentary lives punctuated by binges, broads, and occasional brawls in public places, much to the dismay of their equally cerulean-blooded relatives. TV exposure of Kennedys, Rockefellers, Fords, and so forth, has confirmed middle-class suspicions. To the credit of the breed, the upper crust appears at least minimally repentant.

The **middle class** — always looking upward toward an unattainable notch — has its clay feet. And once you stomp on them, the carefully molded façade shatters from the ground level up. But you have to be quick; the middle class is always on the move. As the Arabs are fond of observing, humankind divides itself into three groups: those that *don't* move, those that *can* move, and those that *move.* And as every hunter knows, the first rabbit to raise its head above the weeds is the least likely to return home with both ears.

Most people reside in the middle class, although with fine shades of distinction. The difference between upper- and lower-middle class, for example, depends upon which newspapers are tossed on their lawns and whether they take vacations at the Holiday Inn or with relatives. Other factors matter, but these two are non-fail, for starters.

All bluffers should proceed on the belief that they are the only truly classless persons among the stratified herd. And never forget that women are *twice* as classy as men.

INTERNATIONAL BLUFF

We were only slightly miffed the other day when an incredibly serious critic indicated his contempt for the Bluffer's Guides because, in his words, "They are riddled with sweeping generalizations." Our reply, issued at high noon with six-guns ablaze, should set the matter straight for future generations of bluffers: "Sweeping generalizations are the life-blood of bluffing." The critic, unable to contrive an appropriate bluff, packed his tattered tent and stole away in the night. A pity, too—we were so looking forward to a rematch.

It's therefore with unrepentent spirit that the following generalizations concerning various nations are offered, beginning with our own kind.

Americans

Americans are *marvelous* people—open-handed, warm-hearted, sincere, and democratic. You'll find your own kind hard to bluff because of our national smile-a-mile-wide flair for bluffery. We Americans have a storehouse of innocently clever remarks, such as "The English are the only people we know who apologize when we step on *their* toes." Not only do Americans freely use the word "bluff," but the term seems to have originated on, or near, Plymouth Rock.

Australians

Australian men are big and burly and fond of ale and sides of mutton. Australian women are even bigger and burlier and make their living in the sheep industry. Australia, apart from the towns around the rim, is mainly empty space inhabited by kangaroos, dingos, koalas, and waltzing Matildas. Australians naturally bluff well, since their ancestors were convicts sent out from England to lessen the population of serious con artists so that less bloodthirsty bluffers would have a chance. Take care with the Aussie bluffer.

French

The French are cocky poseurs and spend most of their waking moments trying to out-do other nations. Their most insidious bluff is the erotic movie, which implies that French sexual prowess deserves international recognition. The French know all about bluffing, which has entered the language through *Franglais*. The French word for bluff is "le bluff," bluffer is "le bluffer," and the idiomatic verb is "faire du bluff." If we don't watch them, they will claim that we stole the whole concept from them.

Germans

Germans, as we all know, cannot be trusted and excel at trying to one-up the rest of the world. They are very good at beer-brewing, wurst-making, and lederhosen-wearing. A good rule of thumb for facing off against a German bluffer is to avoid the ones with the largest tankards of *Bock* and the hairiest knees. The German word for bluff is "der bluff" and the verb is "bluffen" or "verbluffen," depending on the subtlety of the situation.

Spanish

The Spanish, a sulky, sultry lot, in general, think they *ought* to own Gibraltar — which could be described as a bluff at the southwest extremity of Spain. (We had to get the other meaning in somewhere.) The Spanish word for "bluff" is a wonderfully onomatopoetic word, "fanfarronada"; the verb is "fanfarronear"; and a bluffer is a "fanfarron." The Spanish, noted for bull, are said to fanfarronade their way out of most scrapes.

Italians

All Italians should be approached warily, as they live entirely on spaghetti and similar forms of pasta, washing it down with their best wine, which they keep for themselves. They *never* bluff, but are always in dead earnest — particularly in matters of traffic or of the heart. When they pull a stiletto, they *mean* it. Their word for bluffer is "bluffatore."

Swiss

The Swiss are a race of bankers and clock-makers, clinging to the steep inclines of a vertical terrain which foreigners have a passion for sliding down. Their staple diet is a tasteless cheese full of holes. They bluff their way very nicely, thank you, and switch with ease from "le bluff" to "der bluff" and even "bluffatore" before you can decide whether or not to trust them. Probably you shouldn't, unless you're the Pope.

Jews

The Jews used to be the subject of all jokes before people decided to make the butt of their jokes the Irish and then the Poles. The Jewish way of life is based on bluff and counter-bluff, which at varying times has enabled them to stay alive. Anyone who can set up an entire nation adjacent to a nation of hostile Arabs and still keep winning has got a handle on bluffing of inter-national proportions. We wouldn't advise the novice bluffer to venture into their camp.

Poles

The true Pole is a classic case of hypobluffemia, a lack of bluffery. The menfolk, round-cheeked and jolly, like to slap people on the back and dance the polka. The womenfolk, round-cheeked and jolly, don't vary much from the menfolk in behavior or likes and dislikes. Accept the polka as the Polish gift to the world and don't expect much bluffing. Polka-ing jogs all bluf-fery out of the brain, leaving behind its telltale stigma — round cheeks.

Russians

The Russians are a home-and-family-loving nation,

highly proficient in all arts and self-sufficient in everything except ambition. Their character is spoiled only by their belief in practical socialism and their missionary zeal to impose it on everyone else. Russians maintain a high degree of bluff, particularly in personal matters involving the country's output of toilet paper and input of vodka. Cross their frigid borders at your own risk.

Japanese

It is said that the Japanese aren't to be trusted because of their high degree of skill in assimilating (stealing) foreign ideas and marketing them as their own. They spend most of their time designing the biggest TV screens and shortest cars and underpricing everybody else. We are unable, on our old Olympia typewriter, to show you what the Japanese word for "bluff" is, but you can be sure it's closely modeled on ours. And they are masters of the art.

Chinese

Since Marco Polo stole spaghetti and fireworks from the Chinese and began hustling both ideas in the Venice marketplace, the Chinese have become more and more inscrutable, jealously guarding their secrets behind the biggest bluff of all: the Great Wall. As the world's first international bluff, it shows to what length the Chinese will go to out-maneuver their competitors.

AN APOLOGIA

Justifying the Bluff

Bluffing requires skill, dedication, attention to detail, and, above all, personal conviction in order for the devotee to scale the heights of true interpersonal fraudulence. But it's well worth the effort: people will look at you in a new light; the fast-laners or jet-setters (if they really *do* exist outside *The Johnny Carson Show* and glossy magazines) will invite you to their dinner parties; social climbers will cultivate your friendship; and temptresses and gigolos of international repute will slide seductively between your sheets . . . (We can't actually *guarantee* that any of this will happen, but it might.)

Because bluffing has always been an integral part of life in all lands, at all times, and among all levels, it's essential to name some of the heroes, recount once-in-a-lifetime exploits, and draw lessons from these triumphs. As someone must have said by now (probably hotel queen Leona Helmsley), "There isn't a man, woman, or child who has never conned someone out of something." Think about it. A two-year-old smiles to get one more bedtime story, men for a roll in the hay, and women for a diamond and signature on the dotted line.

Here are a few random examples of the bluffer in action:

Great Bluffers

In the 1920s, a Czech nobleman obtained some impressive French government notepaper and used it to invite bids for the Eiffel Tower, to be sold as seven tons of scrap metal. Within two months he sold it twice.

A journalist recently bluffed his way into the Olympic village in Seoul simply by wearing his *1948* Olympic blazer. Korean authorities, eager to save face, refused to let him leave on the inscrutable grounds that because he *shouldn't* be there, he *couldn't* be there. And if he *wasn't* there, how could they let him *out?* As Heller might say, a genuine Catch-22.

America reportedly lost its greatest con man when he died in 1976 in a Chicago nursing home at the age of 100. Serious students rate other claims considerably higher, but this oldtimer was no slouch. He sold "talking dogs," genealogies and family crests, and aluminum siding. On a grander scale, he salted an abandoned quarry with shotgun shells filled with gold and then sold shares in his "gold mine." He treated a stretch of the Colorado River in similar fashion and made a fortune in panning rights. Altogether he must have netted millions, served six years in prison, and made the definitive comment on bluffery: "I never fleeced anyone who couldn't afford my price for a lesson in honesty."

Which raises an issue . . .

It must already be clear that any survey of great bluffers has to deal for the most part with men who have, in legal and ethical terms, gone too far. (We are not espousing sexism. Most master bluffers *have* been men. Women simply must try harder for their place in the scheme of things, no pun intended.) Men have allowed neither restraint, decency, nor a stretch in the slammer to deter them in their pursuit of power, women, promotion, status, fame, material gain, glory, or anything else they want. Not surprisingly, most of them were ruffians and thugs, charlatans and heartless deceivers, swindlers and quacks, forgers and scofflaws, hornswogglers, humbugs, four-flushers, cheats, imposters, frauds, fakes, and assorted scamsters with scarcely two scruples to rub together—a veritable rogues' gallery.

Of course, it's not the aim of the Bluffer's Guides to encourage outright fraud. Fraud is a crime. The cunning bluffer who lurks about these pages is no criminal—make no mistake. Instead, he (or she) is of a kinder and gentler nature—a serious social bluffer who will hopefully learn something about the vast varieties of bluffing styles and techniques from this book.

Still, there are those who *have* made a career out of bluffing, and they claim that any number of unwitting dupes fall victim to their own greed and stupidity. That's probably true. Offered fast bucks and no questions asked, most fools *jump* at the chance. After losing their investment, chumps can't complain too loudly without flaunting their gullibility or allying themselves with shady doings. That's the general pattern.

It can be argued that conning has a salutary effect: the victim, like the Ancient Mariner, goes back to the honest life both sadder and wiser. But to push the matter to its extreme and claim that the fleecer merely gives lessons in ethics and never overcharges the fleecee is blatant bluff and nonsense. It stretches the imagination to suppose that any self-respecting fleecer would pause in mid-fleece to ascertain whether the fleecee can really afford the price — and hold off if the answer is No.

Perhaps it's best to remember a few rules of conduct for bluffers, based on simple maxims; these should be done in needlepoint and hung over every bluffer's mantle:

- There's one born every minute.
- Never give a sucker an even break.
- Take 'em for all you can.
- Forewarned is forearmed.

Such philosophy is reprehensible, of course, but it's realistic, and its wisdom has received support from heavyweights. Nicolo Machiavelli, the beady-eyed theorist of power politics in sixteenth-century Italy, states in his bluffer's masterpiece, *The Prince*

> It's necessary to be a great pretender and dissembler; men are so simple and so subject to present necessities that he who seeks to deceive will always find someone who will allow himself to be deceived. The vulgar are always taken in by what a thing *seems* to be.

This is well-aged wisdom, not to be scoffed at by aspiring bluffers. Machiavelli points to the root truth from which all bluffing springs — the fact that most folk are honest patsies, quite happy to accept you at your own estimation of yourself. IT PAYS TO LAY IT ON THICK.

Winston Churchill, probably England's most eloquent statesman, was all for bluff and deception. "It is not for democracy," he said as he accepted congratulations for Allied landings in North Africa, "to emulate the oyster, serene in its grotto, but rather the blur and smear of the cuttle fish with its dissembling inky fluid."

The accomplished bluffer, for all his moral short-comings, earns the affection of all. Envied and respected for skill, cleverness, and spunk, the bluffer is carried through the marketplace, lifted on high even by the duped themselves, who save their self-respect by admitting that only the best could have bested them.

FOUR KEY BLUFFER QUALITIES

Bluffers, like all natural talents, arrive in this world bearing certain genetic strengths. Among them are these four key qualities (in no particular order):

Quick Wit and a Ready Tongue

Like the natural-born dancer who is light of foot, the bluffer must be naturally light of tongue – ready at the most unassuming opportunity to put on any front and to cover his trail with whatever horse feathers lie at hand. The need for this skill is obvious – no one sets up an appointment to be bluffed. When the time is right, the true bluffer will rise to the occasion with flags flying and all engines on "go."

Example 1

An excellent illustration appears in the Marx Brothers film *A Day at the Races* when Groucho, playing Dr. Hugo Z. Hackenbush, responds to a challenge to his medical credentials. He seizes a nearby wrist, peers intently at his watch for a few seconds, and delivers the clincher: "Either this man is dead or my watch has stopped."

Example 2

Leonard Scabley, a Wall Street scam artist and noted sleaze with a taste for high living, made his nest egg by bilking small sums from thousands of unwitting investors in return for worthless stocks and bonds. Eventually, he met his match and found himself doing a long stretch in Leavenworth. The warden, on a visit to Lenny's prison cell, saw him sewing identification tags on prison linen and remarked, "Well, Lenny, sewing?" "No," came the ready reply, "reaping."

Example 3

English essayist Charles Lamb (who published under the pseudonym of "Elia") spent long hours on a high stool in a boring London office. He hated the job and, approaching retirement, did little to hide his distaste. One day his boss summoned him and snarled, "Do not think that I have failed to notice how late you are arriving for work in the mornings." Lamb replied, "But have you not also noticed how early I depart in the afternoons?"

Example 4

A cub reporter replacing a notorious time-waster on the staff of the *Atlanta Constitution* ended his first interview with a short-tempered boss by asking what had caused the firing of his predecessor. "Well," the grizzled editor snapped, "you might say he departed without leaving a vacancy."

These four examples illustrate the effectiveness of wit, which by sheer unexpectedness and gutsiness, can stop the unwitting dead in their tracks. All great bluffers have it in great measure. One golden fleecer, asked by the judge if he was attempting to show contempt for the court, replied, "No, I'm trying to conceal it."

In a pinch, it's sometimes an effective ploy to answer an awkward question with another question, raising wider philosophical considerations. The first recorded attempt at this method was made by Cain who, having murdered his brother Abel, was unable to explain to the Lord where Abel was. "Am I my brother's keeper?" was the famous response. It didn't work in this case, but it was, under the circumstances, a damn good try. (Even the most accomplished bluffers can hardly hope to get away with it when up against outright omniscience.)

Sheer Audacity

Einstein, Jeane Dixon, and the Ayatollah all share a single principle: audacity. You can achieve anything by audacity. This is a fundamental tenet of the bluffer's creed, based on two self-evident facts: the great majority of people will believe almost anything, and the more outrageous the claim, the more they will be inclined to accept it (succinctly referred to as the "Big Lie" theory). All the great bluffers have operated on this basis.

Example 1

Perhaps the best example took place in 1805 on the great wooden bridge across the Danube at Spitz. The French were on the southern banks of the river, but Austrian infantry and artillery held the northern side, and their engineers had fixed explosives so that the bridge could be destroyed at the first hint of attack.

Two of Napoleon's young Gascon marshals solved the problem of crossing without getting either shot or wet (or both). They put on full-dress uniforms and rode slowly over the bridge in broad daylight, chatting amiably with no sign of hostility. The astonished Austrians held their fire. The commander, who was old and uncommonly dense, met them at the northern end and asked what was going on. "Haven't you heard of the armistice?" they asked. "It's just been signed and the bridge has been handed to us." A long and friendly discussion followed, during the course of which French saboteurs crept up under cover and dismantled the explosives.

The commander was finally persuaded and ordered his troops to fall back. When one of his sergeants cried foul, one of the French marshals demanded, "Is this your famous Austrian discipline, where sergeants countermand generals?" The sergeant soon found himself in the brig. As the French began marching across the bridge, even the Austrian commander started to catch on to the ruse. The two Gascons* reassured him, "They're not advancing—just marking time to keep their feet warm." (*From this illustrious home of superlative bluffers, comes the term "gasconade"—meaning "big talk," or boasting.)

Example 2

"Gutter press" newspapers, such as those found alongside grocery store cash registers, are a bluffer's dream. Ground rules for coverage of completely groundless articles are simple:

(1) The story must be absolutely implausible. Drain the copy of all factual accuracy and capitalize on fantasy—for example, "I Was Impregnated by the Ghost of Elvis" or "My Infant Was Born with a Full Set of Teeth and a Van Dyke Beard."

(2) It must appeal to the depraved and prurient tastes of editors, newswriters, and other undesirables.

As one anonymous regular on the staff of the *National Enquirer* noted, "You've just got to give them something they'll *want* to believe."

Acting Skill

Bluffers are in the illusion business. The best bluffers employ every trick of costume, body language, and razzle-dazzle. Some have been so accomplished that they began to believe their own dog-and-pony show, but such a condition is extremely dangerous—particularly if they're typecast as masochists, hatchet murderers, or extra-terrestrials. Bluffing is something you do to others—never to yourself.

Certain manners and expressions are particularly valuable to the bluffer. They may be categorized as follows:

Expression 1

The air of authority, a *sine qua non* to all great bluffers, must exude from the pores. Here are some notable examples:

(1) A gadfly journalist, making ends meet by guiding tourists around historic Washington, answered

a question from a bosomy Nebraska woman with amazing aplomb. "What do the White House Secret Service men guard?" she asked. With not a moment of hesitation, the journalist replied, "The silver."

(2) A noted faker masqueraded as the Minister of Public Works in the Soviet Union early in the 1970s. He so convinced the bureaucracy of his authenticity that he managed to get an apartment in Moscow, two country houses, and a Mercedes limo—complete with liveried driver. This pseudo-red-tapist wintered in luxury on the Black Sea, whooping it up on vodka, caviar, and other sybaritic delights and never signed a tab. If you have the right manner, it's easier to get away with this sort of thing in rigidly bureaucratic and hierarchical societies. But it's also more dangerous. No one knows what became of the former Minister of Public Works.

(3) Shortly before World War I, a civilian with a grudge made a close study of Prussian army procedures, decked himself out as an officer, commandeered a passing platoon, marched them to town, and arrested the mayor, who had previously done him dirt. Most of Europe got a good yuk out of the caper. (The Prussians, notoriously stiff and stuffy, did not.)

(4) A noted San Francisco practical joker played the old tape trick, enlisting a pedestrian to hold one end of a measuring tape and retreating around the corner to locate a second sucker to hold the other end. Then he retired to a vantage point to

see how long the two boobs would stand there before catching on. This trickster is even more famous for cordoning off a section of the Hollywood Freeway, digging a huge trench across all northbound lanes, and then quietly disappearing.

Expression 2

The ability to remain calm, however threatening the situation, however inevitable it may seem that your bluff is about to be called. A good example is Clifford Irving.

In the early 1970s, the American novelist succeeded in convincing a New York publishing house, McGraw-Hill, and *Life* magazine that he had access to the obsessive-reclusive millionaire Howard Hughes and could furnish them with Hughes's memoirs. Sniffing enormous profits, the greedy bookmen issued Irving enormous advances, the greater part payable to "H. Hughes." These ample gratuities were deposited in a Swiss bank account by Irving's wife, who had foxily adopted the alias "Helga Hughes."

So far, Irving had perpetrated a bold, imaginative, and carefully executed bluff, but his finest moment came when the whole house of cards collapsed around his ears. When reports of the impending book hit the press, Howard Hughes denied any knowledge of Irving *or* the memoirs. Then the Swiss bank revealed that the checks had been endorsed by a woman. There was further incriminating evidence. The future of Irving's bluffing looked bleak. A lesser bluffer would have cut and run, but not Irving. He flew to New York, confronted his skeptical publishers, fielded their questions with a wealth of trumped-up detail, then mounted the podium with his trickery well in hand:

> "There are three possibile explanations. First, that I've been dealing all along with an imposter. Second, that Hughes, for his own inscrutable purposes, used a loyal servant to cash his checks for him. Third, that I am a hoaxer. The last of these possibilities I discard out of hand. And I trust that you will do likewise."

The assemblage nodded and continued issuing checks for several more weeks before they realized they'd been had—on a colossal scale.

Attention to Minutiae

Bluffer satisfaction grows in inverse proportion to the effort involved: the lower the merit, in terms of real knowledge or experience or thought, the better the bluffing has to be to insure success.

This paradigm should not, however, be taken to imply that the good bluffer is entirely ignorant of everything except the techniques of bluffery. It pays to have at least a smattering of genuine knowledge, which is where the Bluffer's Guides come in handy. And it can sometimes pay handsomely to have a real command of some narrow and esoteric subject, such as oboe repair or medieval bookbinding or truffle farming. Houdini, as you will recall if you saw the movie, speaks approvingly of "corroborative detail, intended to give artistic verisimilitude to an otherwise bald and unconvincing artifice." Many master bluffers have recognized the importance of this single essential.

Example 1

Bella Gregory (an acclaimed Texas attorney), when she was house-hunting outside Dallas, demanded that the exterior be white. This forethought allowed her to answer calls at a number of public places where she tipped flunkies to interrupt her *tête-à-têtes* with potential clients and announce, "The White House is on the phone, Bella. Shall I have them call back?" Conversation, needless to say, came to a dead halt as Bella weighed the importance of the call and then rejected it in favor of more pressing matters—the latest easy pickings. Need we say, she was the darling of the litigious set?

Example 2

"The Man Who Never Was," the brainchild of an unsung naval intelligence officer during the Vietnam War, developed into full-fledged personhood during the mining of Haiphong Harbor. The aim was to deceive the Viet Cong that Lyndon Johnson intended to bottle up strategic defenses in order to launch a land-sea-and-air invasion massive enough to wind up the war with a classic blitzkrieg.

This chicanery depended upon the remains of an American brigadier-general, carrying phony letters to Command Central in Saigon, being washed up on the Vietnamese coast. Even though American adjutants denied any knowledge of the purported officer, Viet Cong watchdogs swept the entire Southeast Asian coastline for weeks, throwing all their fire power toward the phantom invasion. Who knows, they may still be waiting.

THE MASTER

The eighteenth century produced one of the all-time greats of the game, perhaps the first man to earn a regular living and considerable fame from bluffery. He called himself Georges Psalmanazar. It isn't known where he got the "Georges," but he took the surname from an Assyrian king of dubious character. The unlikely name was sufficiently impressive for his purposes. (Sometimes he spelled it with as many as six *a*'s scattered about, but finally settled for the version used here.)

A man of many mysteries, largely arising from the fact that as he was the sole source of data about his early years, he was not entirely reliable. The year 1679 is the usual date given for his birth. It's not known where he originated, although Rhode Island often claims him (France does too, however). Early on, he demonstrated two auspicious idiosyncrasies—a passion for notoriety and a gift for languages. Among leading bluffers, all have had the former and a surprisingly high percentage have had the latter.

Sometime in his mid-teens, Georges went to Germany, where he began to evolve an immense sham: he posed as an unconverted savage, observing lurid, barbaric rites in a ragged loincloth and using sackfuls of feathers, tallow, and an occasional virgin. From there, he traveled to England, where (with the aid of an even more clever bluffer, a Scottish chaplain named

Bill Inness) he quickly became an Instant Celebrity (like Michael Jackson's new face or the Elephant Man). He created his own language, babbled away in it fluently, and devised an alphabet for it, producing "Formosan" manuscripts. (Bill had suggested that Georges' native country be the then-exotic Formosa.) Georges-the-converted-Formosan was the sensation of London's social season for three years' running: 1704–06. The Bishop of London saw to his every need, and scientists and historians fawned over him. Cannibalism, Georges said, was not a sin; it was only "unmannerly."

"His assurance," someone wrote, "silenced suspicions of fraud." He made it a practice never to withdraw or modify any assertion. Challenged to prove his Formosan ancestry, his prompt response stands as the all-time object lesson to aspiring bluffers:

"How *can* I? If you, sir, arrived on my island and my fellow Formosans said, 'Prove to us that you are English,' how would you do it? They would think that you looked like some French trapper or some American bead-and-trinket trader; they would have no notion of what an Englishman looks like."

Now *that* is bluffing on a grand scale!